EASY PIANO

THE Best
IN CHRISTMAS SHEET MUSIC

ARRANGED BY DAN COATES

Dan Coates

One of today's foremost personalities in the field of printed music, Dan Coates has been providing teachers and professional musicians with quality piano material since 1975. Equally adept in arranging for beginners or accomplished musicians, his Big Note, Easy Piano and Professional Touch arrangements have made a significant contribution to the industry.

Born in Syracuse, New York, Dan began to play piano at age four. By the time he was 15, he'd won a New York State competition for music composers. After high school graduation, he toured the United States, Canada and Europe as an arranger and pianist with the world-famous group "Up With People".

Dan settled in Miami, Florida, where he studied piano with Ivan Davis at the University of Miami while playing professionally throughout southern Florida. To date, his performance credits include appearances on "Murphy Brown," "My Sister Sam" and at the Opening Ceremonies of the 1984 Summer Olympics in Los Angeles. Dan has also accompanied such artists as Dusty Springfield and Charlotte Rae.

In 1982, Dan began his association with Warner Bros. Publications - an association which has produced more than 400 Dan Coates books and sheets. Throughout the year he conducts piano workshops nation-wide, during which he demonstrates his popular arrangements.

CONTENTS

ALL I WANT FOR CHRISTMAS IS MY TWO FRONT TEETH

Words and Music by
DON GARDNER
Arranged by DAN COATES

All I want for Christ-mas is my two front teeth, my two front teeth, see my two front teeth! Gee, if I could on-ly have my two front teeth, then I could wish you, "Mer-ry Christ-mas." It seems so long since I could say, "Sis-ter Su-sie sit-ting on a

DECK THE HALL

Traditional Old Welsh
Arranged by DAN COATES

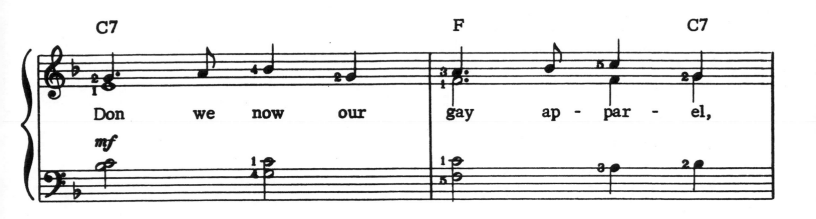

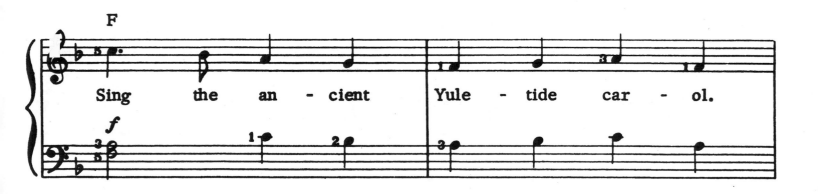

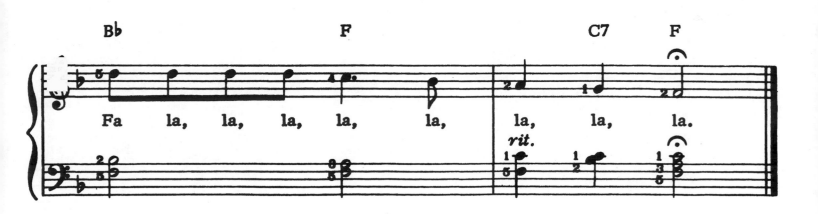

GESU BAMBINO
(The Infant Jesus)

Words by
FREDERICK H. MARTENS

Music by
PIETRO A. YON
Arranged by DAN COATES

HAVE YOURSELF
A MERRY LITTLE CHRISTMAS

Words and Music by
HUGH MARTIN and
RALPH BLANE
Arranged by **DAN COATES**

GOD REST YE MERRY, GENTLEMEN

Traditional English Carol
Arranged by DAN COATES

Chorus

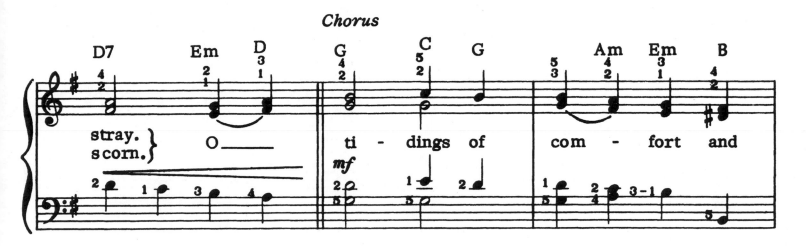

O_____ ti - dings of com - fort and

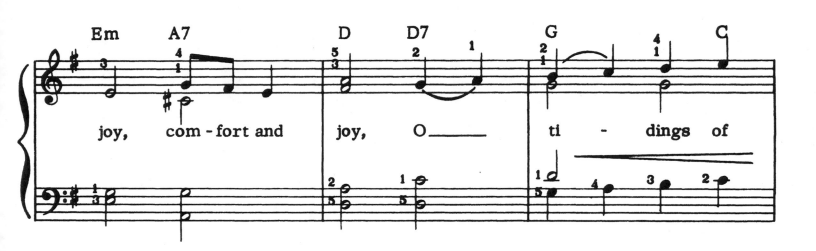

joy, com - fort and joy, O_____ ti - dings of

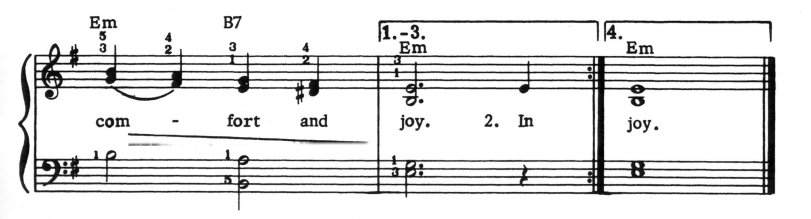

com - fort and joy. 2. In | joy.

Additional Lyrics

3. From God our Heavenly Father, a blessed Angel came;
   And unto certain shepherds, brought tidings of the same;
   How that in Bethlehem was born the Son of God by name.

   (Chorus)

4. The shepherds at those tidings rejoiced much in mind,
   And left their flocks a-feeding, in tempest, storm, and wind,
   And went to Bethlehem straight-way, the Son of God to find.

   (Chorus)

HARK! THE HERALD ANGELS SING

Words by
CHARLES WESLEY

Music by
FELIX MENDELSSOHN
Arranged by DAN COATES

A HOLLY JOLLY CHRISTMAS

Words and Music by
JOHNNY MARKS
Arranged by DAN COATES

IT'S THE MOST WONDERFUL TIME OF THE YEAR

By
EDDIE POLA and GEORGE WYLE
Arranged by DAN COATES

24

JINGLE BELLS

Traditional
Arranged by DAN COATES

JOLLY OLD ST. NICHOLAS

Anonymous
Arranged by DAN COATES

THE LITTLE DRUMMER BOY

Words and Music by
KATHERINE DAVIS, HENRY ONORATI
and HARRY SIMEONE
Arranged by DAN COATES

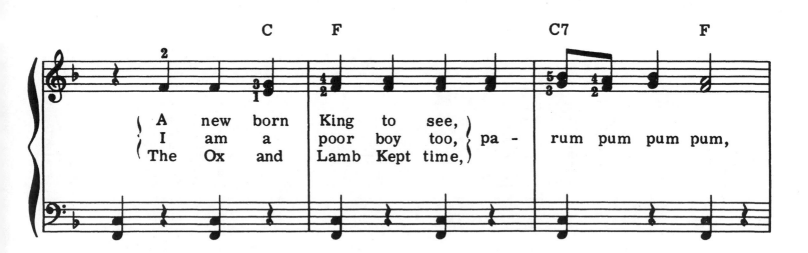

LET IT SNOW! LET IT SNOW! LET IT SNOW!

Lyric by
SAMMY CAHN

Music by
JULE STYNE
Arranged by DAN COATES

MERRY CHRISTMAS, DARLING

Lyrics by
FRANK POOLER

Music by
RICHARD CARPENTER
Arranged by DAN COATES

THE MOST WONDERFUL DAY OF THE YEAR

Words and Music by
JOHNNY MARKS
Arranged by DAN COATES

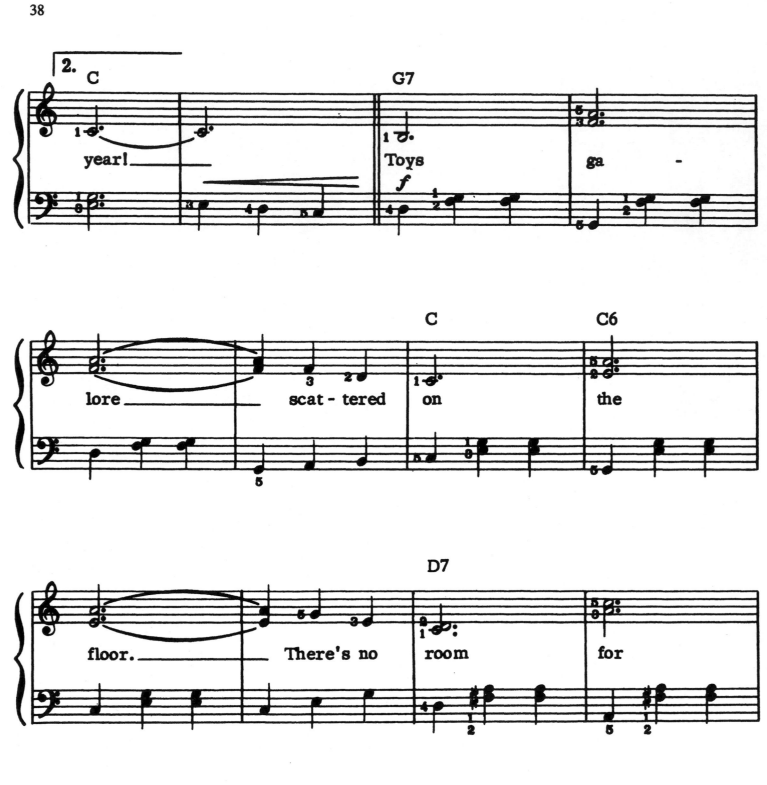

year! _____ Toys ga -

lore _____ scat - tered on the

floor. _____ There's no room for

more, _____ and it's all be - cause of

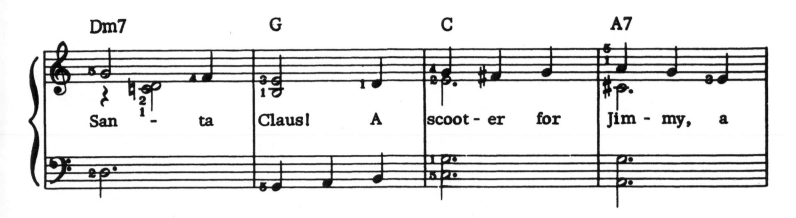

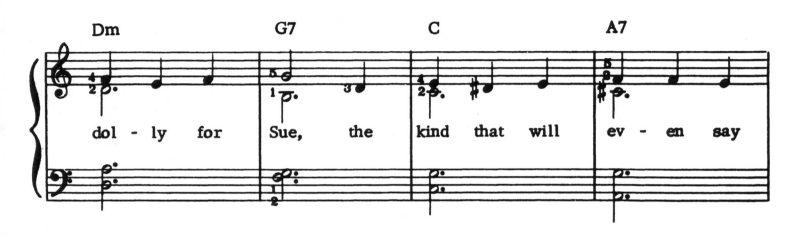

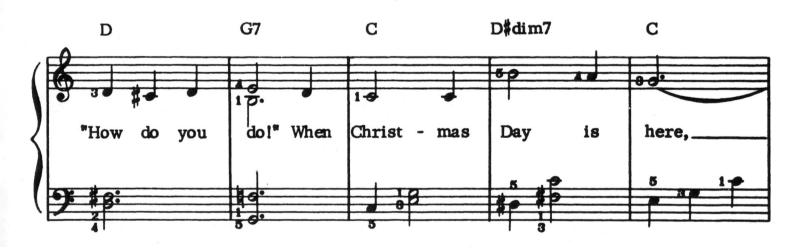

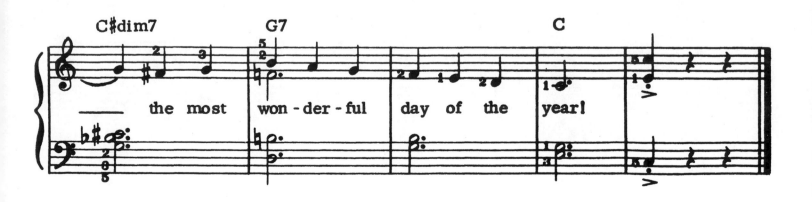

O COME, O COME EMMANUEL

Traditional
Arranged by DAN COATES

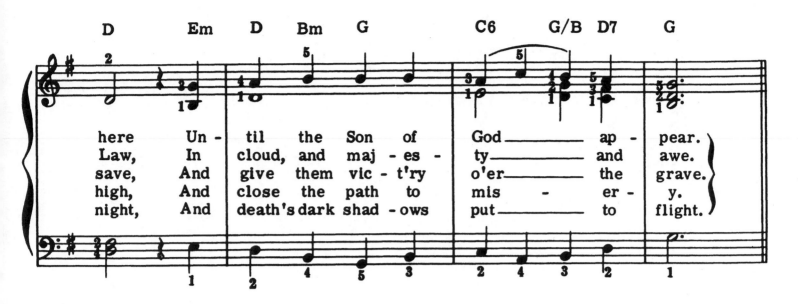

here Un - til the Son of God _____ ap - pear.
Law, In cloud, and maj - es - ty _____ and awe.
save, And give them vic - t'ry o'er _____ the grave.
high, And close the path to mis - er - y.
night, And death's dark shad - ows put _____ to flight.

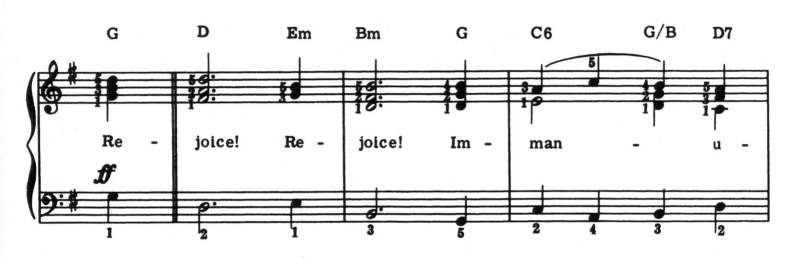

Re - joice! Re - joice! Im - man - u -

el Shall come to thee, O Is - ra - el.

ROCKIN' AROUND
THE CHRISTMAS TREE

Words and Music by
JOHNNY MARKS
Arranged by DAN COATES

Moderately, with a rock

ring. Lat-er we'll have some pump-kin pie __ and we'll

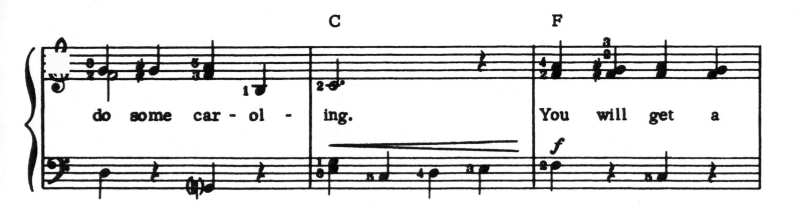

do some car - ol - ing. You will get a

sen - ti - men - tal feel - ing when you hear

voic - es sing - ing, "Let's be jol - ly, deck the halls with

RUDOLPH, THE RED-NOSED REINDEER

Words and Music by
JOHNNY MARKS
Arranged by DAN COATES

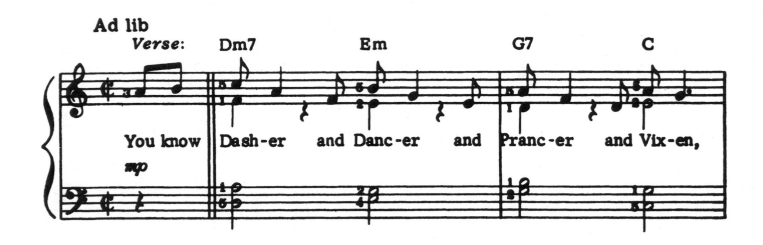

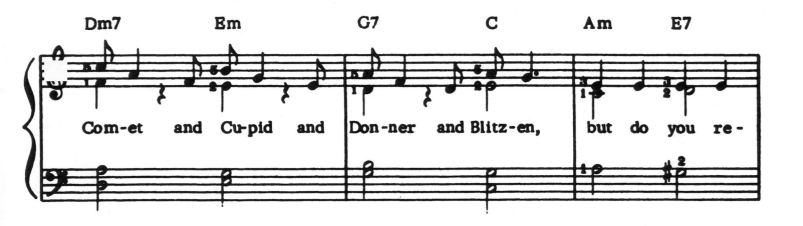

Lightly
Chorus:

SANTA CLAUS IS COMIN' TO TOWN

Words by
HAVEN GILLESPIE

Music by
J. FRED COOTS
Arranged by DAN COATES

SILENT NIGHT

Words by
JOSEPH MOHR

Music by
FRANZ GRUBER
Arranged by DAN COATES

SLEIGH RIDE

Words by
MITCHELL PARISH

Music by
LEROY ANDERSON
Arranged by DAN COATES

THE TWELVE DAYS OF CHRISTMAS

Old English
Arranged by DAN COATES

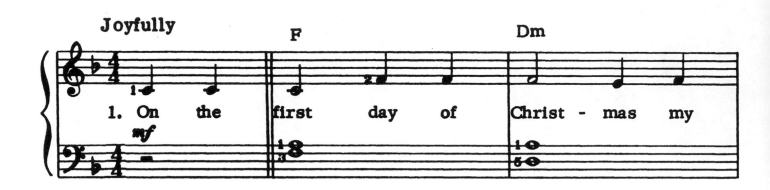

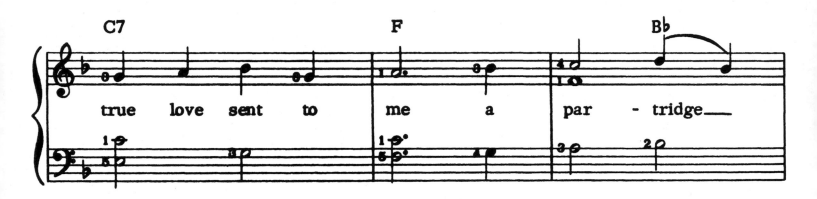

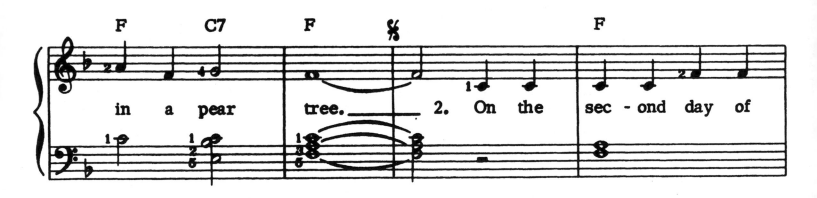

two tur - tle doves and a par - tridge___
(Repeat 2nd and 3rd times)

D. S. for Verses 3 and 4

in a pear tree.___ 5. On the fifth day of

Christ - mas, my true love sent to me five

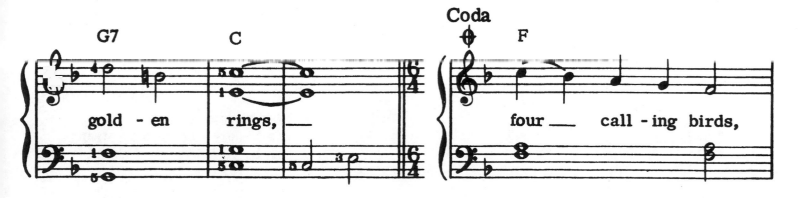

Coda

gold - en rings,___ four___ call - ing birds,

three French hens, two___ tur - tle doves, and a

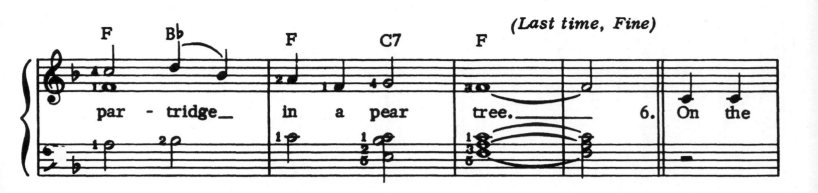

3. On the third ⎤
4. On the fourth ⎦ day of Christmas, my true love sent to me ⎡ two turtle doves ⎤ and a part-
                                                                    ⎢ three French hens ⎥ ridge in a
                                                                    ⎣ four calling birds ⎦ pear tree.

6. On the sixth
7. On the seventh
8. On the eighth
9. On the ninth   day of Christmas, my true love sent to me ⎡ six geese a-laying, ⎤
10. On the tenth   ⎢ seven swans-a-swimming, ⎥
11. On the 'leventh   ⎢ eight maids a-milking, ⎥ five
12. On the twelfth   ⎢ nine ladies dancing, ⎥ golde
                                                           ⎢ ten lords a-leaping, ⎥ rings
                                                           ⎢ 'leven pipers piping, ⎥
                                                           ⎣ twelve drummers drumming, ⎦

WE WISH YOU A
MERRY CHRISTMAS

Traditional English Folk Song
Arranged by DAN COATES

WE THREE KINGS
OF ORIENT ARE

Traditional
Arranged by DAN COATES

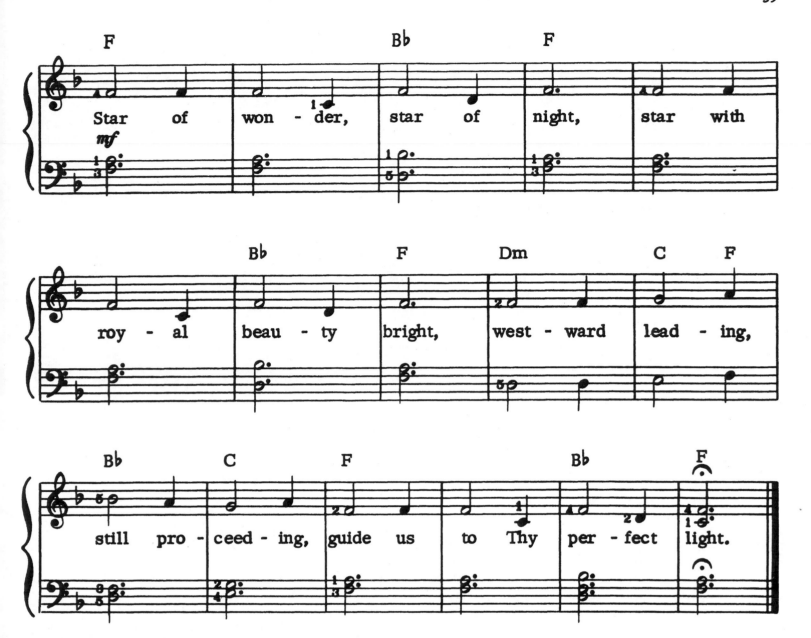

Additional Lyrics

2. Born a King on Bethlehem's plain,
Gold I bring, to crown Him again,
King forever, ceasing never
Over us all to reign:

3. Frankincense to offer have I,
Incense owns a Deity nigh.
Prayer and praising, all men raising
Worship Him, God most high:

4. Myrrh is mine, its bitter perfume
Breathes a life of gathering gloom;
Sorrowing, sighing, bleeding, dying,
Sealed in the stone-cold tomb:

5. Glorious now behold Him arise,
King and God and sacrifice!
Heaven sings Alleluia,
Alleluia the earth replies:

O COME, ALL YE FAITHFUL
(Adeste Fideles)

By
JOHN FRANCIS WADE
Arranged by **DAN COATES**

Moderate, steady tempo

O come, all ye faith - ful,

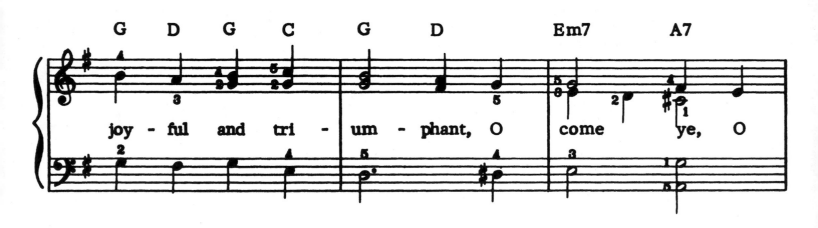

joy - ful and tri - um - phant, O come ye, O

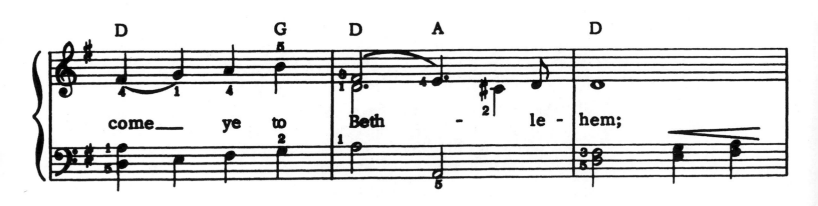

come___ ye to Beth - le - hem;

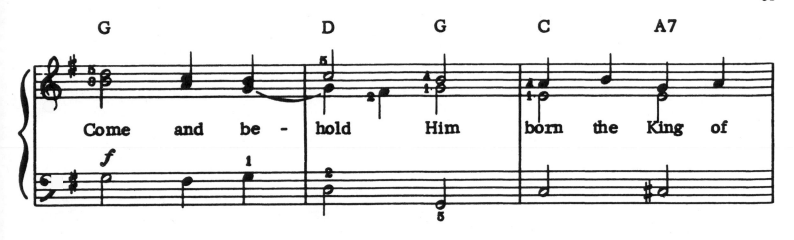

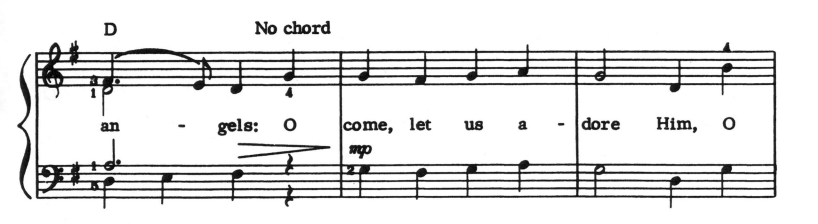

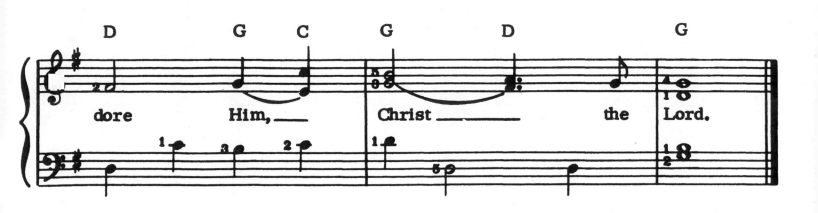

WINTER WONDERLAND

Words by
DICK SMITH

Music by
FELIX BERNARD
Arranged by DAN COATES

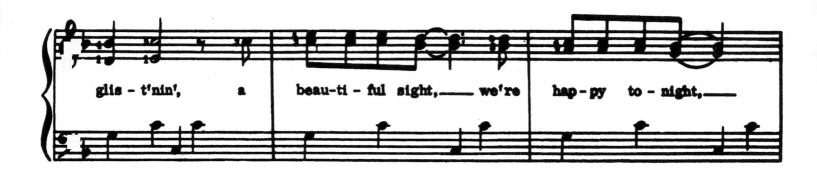

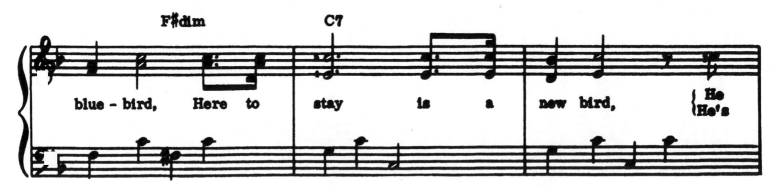

sings a love song,—} as we go a-long,—— walk-in' in a win-ter won-der-
sing-ing a song,—}

land! In the mea-dow we can build a snow-man,

{Then pre-tend that he is Par-son Brown;
{And pre-tend that he's a cir-cus clown;

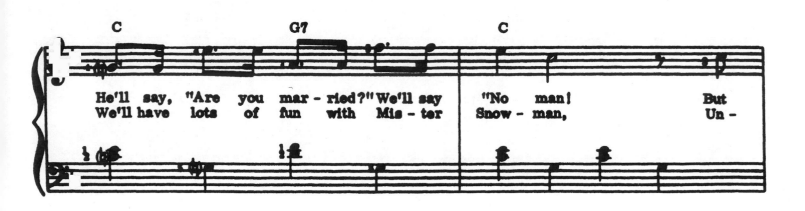

He'll say, "Are you mar-ried?" We'll say "No man! But
We'll have lots of fun with Mis-ter Snow-man, Un-

you can do   the job   when you're in | town!"   Lat - er
til   the oth - er   kid - dies knock 'im | down!   When   it

on.   we'll con - | spire,____   As   we | dream   by   the
snows,   ain't   it | thrill - in',   Though your | nose   gets   a

fire,____   To | face un - a - fraid, the | plans that we   made,}
chill - in' ?   We'll | frol - ic and play the | es - ki - mo way,}

walk - in' in   a   win - ter won-der- | land!   Sleigh bells | land!